NATIONAL MALL

Joanne Mattern

Rourke
Educational Media

rourkeeducationalmedia.com

Before Reading:

Building Academic Vocabulary and Background Knowledge

Before reading a book, it is important to tap into what your child or students already know about the topic. This will help them develop their vocabulary, increase their reading comprehension, and make connections across the curriculum.

1. *Look at the cover of the book. What will this book be about?*
2. *What do you already know about the topic?*
3. *Let's study the Table of Contents. What will you learn about in the book's chapters?*
4. *What would you like to learn about this topic? Do you think you might learn about it from this book? Why or why not?*
5. *Use a reading journal to write about your knowledge of this topic. Record what you already know about the topic and what you hope to learn about the topic.*
6. *Read the book.*
7. *In your reading journal, record what you learned about the topic and your response to the book.*
8. *After reading the book complete the activities below.*

Content Area Vocabulary
Read the list. What do these words mean?

architect
artifacts
civil rights
engineer
envisioned
granite
marble
mementos
memorial
monument
obelisk

After Reading:

Comprehension and Extension Activity

After reading the book, work on the following questions with your child or students in order to check their level of reading comprehension and content mastery.

1. *Who designed the National Mall and why was he not involved in the process? (Summarize)*
2. *Why does Abraham Lincoln have a memorial? (Asking questions)*
3. *What museums, memorials, and monuments do you want to visit? (Text to self connection)*
4. *How was the Smithsonian created? (Summarize)*
5. *What are artifacts? (Summarize)*

Extension Activity

The National Mall has numerous museums, memorials, statues, and parks. Research one of the points of interest. Create a brochure using a computer program or a tri-folded piece of paper. On your brochure include the history, fun facts, reasons why it was constructed, pictures, location, and other points of interest. Share your brochure with a classmate.

TABLE OF CONTENTS

WELCOME TO THE NATIONAL MALL!

Welcome to America's front yard! That is just one nickname for the National Mall. This beautiful and special place has also been called "the Great Park of the American people." It is a wonderful place to explore and discover America's history.

The Korean War Veterans Memorial

The National Mall is located in Washington, D.C. It is a place of monuments, museums, gardens, and open spaces. There are sculptures and statues along the National Mall, as well as quiet places of great beauty. You'll even find a castle on the Mall! Wherever you are, there is always something to discover.

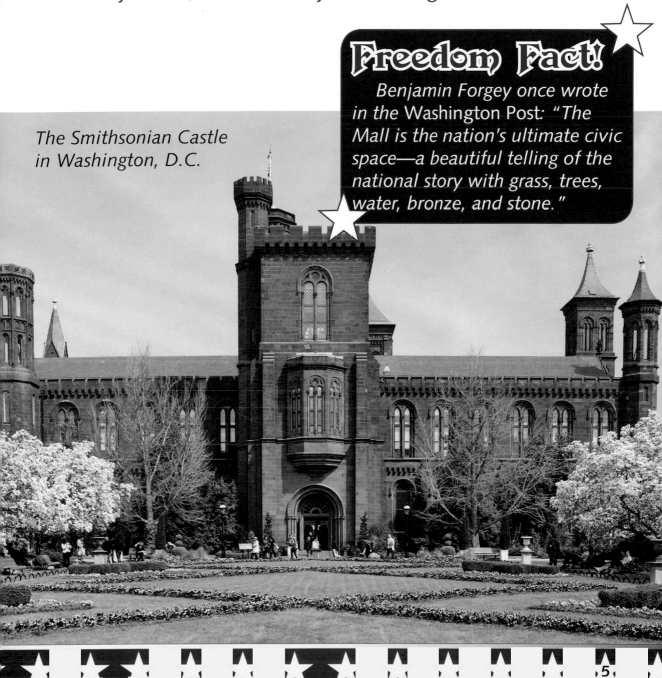

The Smithsonian Castle in Washington, D.C.

Freedom Fact!

Benjamin Forgey once wrote in the Washington Post: "The Mall is the nation's ultimate civic space—a beautiful telling of the national story with grass, trees, water, bronze, and stone."

The National Mall is shaped like a long rectangle. It is located in the middle of busy city streets in our nation's capital. Constitution Avenue marks the northern border of the Mall, while Independence Avenue marks the southern border. The Mall begins at First Street in the east and runs almost to the edge of the Potomac River in the west. Altogether, the Mall stretches for a little less than two miles (3.2 kilometers).

Many monuments and attractions are located on the National Mall.

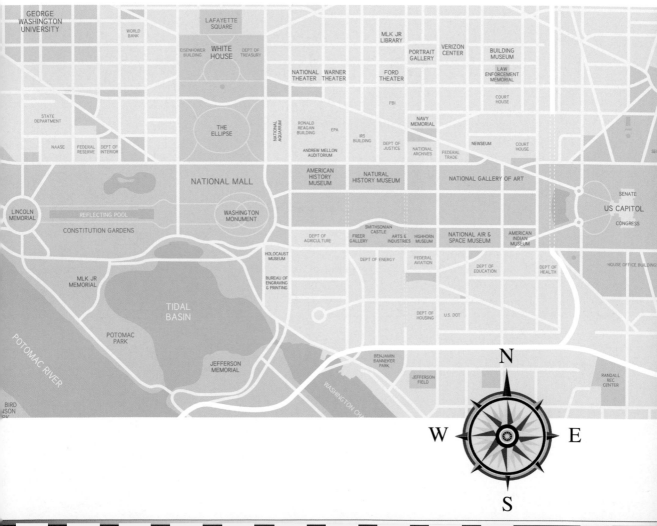

Because the National Mall is located in the heart of Washington, D.C., many famous buildings surround it. The U.S. Capitol and the U.S. Supreme Court buildings are located to the east of the Mall. The White House, home of the president, is also located near the National Mall.

Freedom Fact!

More than 25 million people from all over the world visit the National Mall each year.

U.S. Supreme Court Building

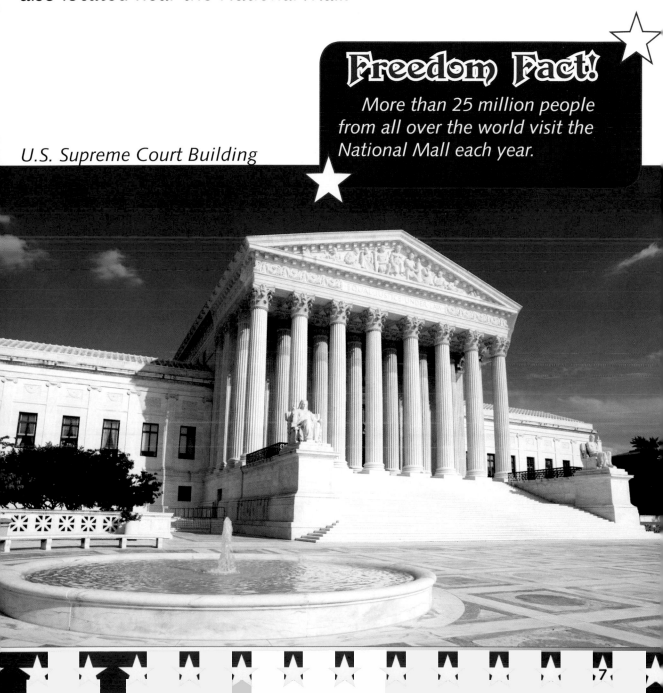

PIERRE L'ENFANT

The idea for the National Mall came from a French native. Pierre Charles L'Enfant was born in France in 1754 and grew up to be an artist and an **engineer**. In 1777, he left France to join American troops in the American Revolution.

During the war, L'Enfant became friends with George Washington. When Washington announced that a new United States capital city would be built along the banks of the Potomac River, L'Enfant asked if he could help create a plan for the city. Washington said yes, and in March 1791, L'Enfant was hired to prepare plans for the city.

Freedom Fact!

*L'Enfant also created 15 large, open spaces where the city's avenues intersected. He **envisioned** that each of the current 15 states would use these spaces to build statues honoring their most important citizens.*

L'Enfant visited the site of the new city and was overwhelmed by the beautiful view. He was so excited to start working that he drew up plans even before the government gave him a contract. L'Enfant placed the Capitol building on high ground, overlooking the city. Long, wide, tree-lined avenues spread across the city. An especially large avenue would connect the Capitol and the president's house. The streets would connect with other sites in the area where monuments, fountains, and other structures would be built one day.

L'Enfant also planned a grassy area called a mall that would stretch about one mile (1.6 kilometers) away from the Capitol, ending at a **monument** to his friend, President Washington.

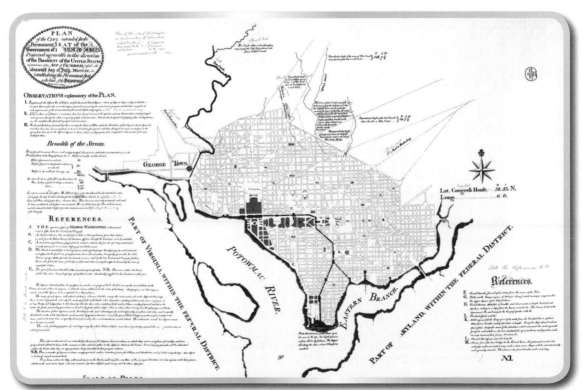

A reproduction of Pierre Charles L'Enfant's plans show what he imagined for the city of Washington.

L'Enfant's plans were well-liked, but unfortunately L'Enfant was not. He had a bad temper and refused to compromise. On March 1, 1792, Washington dismissed L'Enfant from his position as design **architect**. However, L'Enfant's plans were still used to build the city.

George Washington (1732–1799)

George Washington commanded the U.S. Army during the American Revolution and later became our nation's first president.

At first, the grassy area called the National Mall was used only to grow crops and graze cattle. Public markets were held on the Mall, and railroad tracks were even laid across it. But, in 1901, everything changed. A Senate committee met to redesign the nation's capital. The architects decided to extend the Mall all the way to the Potomac River and build a **memorial** to President Abraham Lincoln.

Pierre L'Enfant died long before the Mall turned into the beautiful place it is today. However, without his ideas and plans, our nation's capital would look very different.

Pierre L'Enfant's grave is located in Arlington National Cemetery.

MONUMENTS AND MEMORIALS

Some of the most famous and important places on the National Mall are the monuments that honor individuals or memorialize important events. The National Mall is home to some of the most famous monuments in the United States.

The Washington Monument

The Washington Monument was the first major memorial built on the Mall. In 1833, the Washington National Monument Society held a contest to come up with a design. Robert Mills won the contest. His plan called for a 600-foot-tall (183-meter) **obelisk** surrounded by columns topped with a statue of George Washington.

Freedom Fact!

Only Congress can allow a monument to be built on the Mall.

It took a long time to raise the money to build the monument. In 1880, a new designer named Colonel Thomas L. Casey got rid of the columns and the statue. Instead, only the obelisk stands as a memorial to our first president. The Washington Monument finally opened in 1885.

The Washington Monument is made of blocks of **marble** from Maryland and Massachusetts. It stands just over 555 feet (196 meters) tall and weighs 90,854 tons (82,421 metric tons). Visitors can take a thrilling elevator ride to the top and see amazing views of the National Mall and the city. A long, rectangular pool, called the Reflecting Pool, lies in front of the Monument.

The Lincoln Memorial

Abraham Lincoln is considered one of the greatest U.S. presidents. To honor him, the Lincoln Memorial was built in 1922. The Lincoln Memorial looks like a Greek temple. The building has 36 columns around a memorial chamber, one for every state at that time. Inside is a huge statue of Abraham Lincoln. The statue measures 19 feet (5.8 meters) high and sits on an 11-foot-tall (3.3-meter) pedestal. Carved into the marble above the statue it reads: "In this temple, as in the hearts of the people for whom he saved the Union, the memory of Abraham Lincoln is enshrined forever."

The building is in the form of a Greek Doric temple and contains a large seated sculpture of Abraham Lincoln.

On August 28, 1963, Martin Luther King, Jr., stood on the steps of the Lincoln Memorial and gave one of the most important speeches in American history. Hundreds of thousands of people of all races filled the space between the Lincoln Memorial and the Washington Memorial to hear King's famous "I Have a Dream" speech. His words became one of the most important moments in the **civil rights** movement.

More than 250,000 people came to the National Mall to hear Martin Luther King, Jr. speak.

The Vietnam Veterans Memorial

The Vietnam Veterans Memorial is just 600 feet (183 meters) away from the Lincoln Memorial. It honors the men and women who served in the Vietnam War. A long wall made of black **granite** has the names of more than 58,000 servicemen and women carved into it. These brave men and women either died in the war or are still missing.

*Millions of people visit the Vietnam Veterans Memorial each year. Many leave gifts, photos, or other **mementos** there.*

The Vietnam War was not a popular war, and the memorial was not popular at first either. A young college student named Maya Lin won a national competition to design the monument, which opened in 1982. At first, people hated her work and thought the black wall was not heroic enough to honor the soldiers. However, the simple and overwhelming sight of all those names carved into the black granite soon showed people the power of the monument. Since it opened, the Vietnam Veterans Memorial has been called one of the greatest war memorials in the world.

The National Mall has many other monuments to honor soldiers, presidents, and other American heroes. Here are some of the Mall's monuments and memorials:

★ African-American Civil War Memorial
★ Constitution Gardens
★ District of Columbia War Memorial
★ East Potomac Park
★ Ford's Theatre National Historic Site and the House Where Lincoln Died
★ Franklin Delano Roosevelt Memorial
★ Hispanic Heroes on Virginia Avenue, NW
★ Japanese American Memorial to Patriotism during World War II
★ Korean War Veterans Memorial
★ Lincoln Memorial
★ Martin Luther King, Jr. Memorial
★ National Law Enforcement Officers Memorial
★ Old Post Office Tower
★ Pennsylvania Avenue National Historic Site and Park
★ Thomas Jefferson Memorial
★ Vietnam Veterans Memorial
★ Washington Monument
★ West Potomac Park
★ World War II Memorial

Freedom Fact!

The Martin Luther King, Jr. Memorial was added to the National Mall in 2011.

MUSEUMS AND A CASTLE!

There is a lot more to see on the National Mall than monuments and statues! The Mall is also home to the largest and most fascinating museum in the world: the Smithsonian Institution. It includes 16 museums and art galleries. Nine of these buildings are located on the National Mall.

James Smithson was a wealthy English scientist who died in 1829. Even though he had never visited the United States, Smithson left his entire fortune of more than $500,000, a huge sum in 1829, to the United States. In his will, Smithson explained that he wanted the money used "to found at Washington, under the name of the Smithsonian Institution, an establishment for the increase and diffusion of knowledge."

The U.S. Congress wasn't quite sure what to do with this gift. For many years, Congressmen argued about how to use the money. Finally, on August 10, 1846, President James Polk signed a bill to create the Smithsonian Institution. The Institution would be dedicated to research and to providing information to the public. It would also be a place to store and display America's treasures. Years later, the famous American author Mark Twain called the Smithsonian "America's Attic."

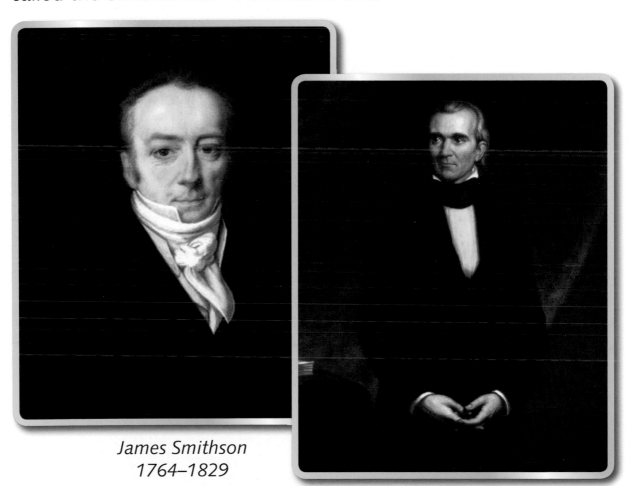

James Smithson
1764–1829

James Polk
1795–1849

The Smithsonian Building was the first building. It was completed in 1855 and originally held the Institution's entire collection of **artifacts** and exhibits. The building was made of red sandstone and designed to look like a European castle. Today, it is simply called the Castle and serves as an information center for visitors.

Smithsonian Building, Castle

The Arts and Industries Building was the second Smithsonian building. It opened in 1881 and was originally called the National Museum. That is a good name, because the building holds many fascinating exhibits and collections. Later, when the collection got too big, it was spread out into other buildings.

The Arts and Industries Building

The Smithsonian Institution also includes several art galleries. These galleries include the Hirshhorn Museum, which houses modern art; the Freer Gallery of Art and the Arthur M. Sackler Gallery, which include Asian art; and the National Museum of African Art.

The National Museum of American History may be the most interesting and amazing part of the Smithsonian. This museum tells the story of our nation's history and culture. Along with historical artifacts, such as the flag that inspired "The Star-Spangled Banner," there are also items that reflect popular culture, such as Dorothy's ruby slippers from *The Wizard of Oz*, a signed baseball from the 1937 All-Star Game, and an original Kermit the Frog Muppet.

Pieces of "The Star Spangled Banner"   *Dorothy's ruby slippers*

Would you like to see the original plane that the Wright Brothers flew back in 1903? How about the *Apollo 11 Command Module* or a test vehicle from the *Hubble Space Telescope*? All of these historic vehicles and many more are on display at the National Air and Space Museum. Like the artifacts and art in the other buildings of the Smithsonian Institution, the exhibits at the Air and Space Museum show important moments in America's history. They allow people to experience the events that made the United States the nation it is today.

Macchi C202 and Mustang P-51D

Freedom Fact!

The National Air and Space Museum also includes hundreds of model airplanes.

GARDENS AND OPEN SPACES

There is so much to see on the National Mall that visitors sometimes want to escape and find some peace and quiet. Pierre L'Enfant understood that, and his original plans for the National Mall included plenty of open space.

The Mall includes miles of tree-lined paths that are perfect for walking, jogging, or bicycling. There is also a great stretch of open grass between the Capitol Building and the Washington Monument. This area

has become a true people's park, where people enjoy picnics, play ball, fly kites, or run with their dogs.

The Enid A. Haupt Garden is the most famous garden on the Mall. The garden is filled with several acres of flowers laid out in patterns. Different parts of the garden feature different flowers.

A quiet park called Constitution Gardens is another popular spot. It lies along Constitution Avenue between the Washington Monument and the Lincoln Memorial. The gardens include trees and a pond, and it is a favorite spot for bird watchers.

The Constitution Gardens gives tourists a serene and quiet place to observe the Mall.

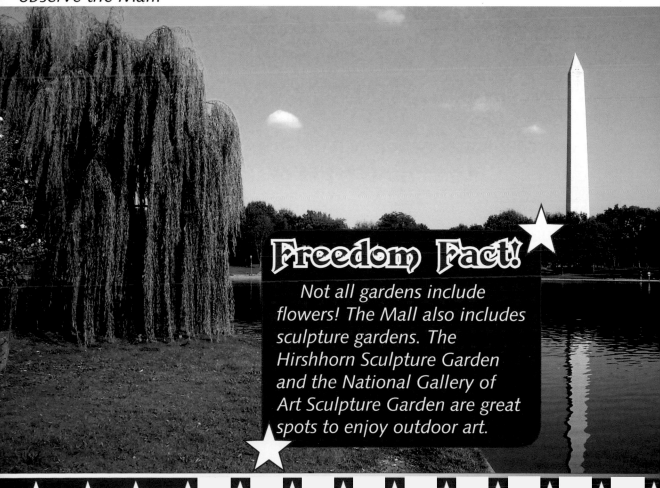

Freedom Fact!

Not all gardens include flowers! The Mall also includes sculpture gardens. The Hirshhorn Sculpture Garden and the National Gallery of Art Sculpture Garden are great spots to enjoy outdoor art.

Millions of people visit the National Mall each year. The Mall is open twenty-four hours a day, and it is not unusual for visitors to linger there after dark. Most of the monuments are also open late, and park rangers are available to guide visitors during most of the day and evening. If you can't get to Washington, D.C., you can explore the National Mall and the Smithsonian Institution online.

Visit America's front yard, and see the places that symbolize some of the greatest moments and people in American history.

Freedom Fact!

The National Park Service runs the National Mall, which is part of the federal government.

TIMELINE

1791 —— *Pierre Charles L'Enfant draws up plans for Washington, D.C.*

1829 —— *James Smithson leaves his fortune to the United States to start the Smithsonian Institution.*

1846 —— *The Smithsonian Institution is created.*

1855 —— *The Smithsonian Building opens.*

1881 —— *The Arts and Industry Building opens.*

1885 —— *The Washington Monument opens.*

1901 —— *A committee meets to redesign the nation's capital.*

1922 —— *The Lincoln Memorial is built.*

1963 —— *Martin Luther King, Jr. delivers his "I Have a Dream" speech from the steps of the Lincoln Memorial.*

1982 —— *The Vietnam Veterans Memorial opens.*

1999 —— *The National Gallery of Art Sculpture Garden opens.*

2011 —— *The Martin Luther King, Jr. Memorial opens.*

GLOSSARY

architect (AR-ki-tekt): someone who designs buildings

artifacts (ART-uh-fakts): objects made or changed by humans

civil rights (SIV-il RITES): the rights that all members of society have to equal treatment

engineer (en-juh-NEER): someone who is trained to design or build machines or structures

envisioned (en-VIZH-uhnd): imagined something for the future

granite (GRAN-it): a hard, gray rock

marble (MAR-buhl): a hard stone with colored patterns in it

mementos (muh-MEN-tohs): small items kept to remember a place, person, or event

memorial (muh-MOR-ee-uhl): something built or done to help people remember a person or event

monument (MON-yuh-muhnt): a statue, building, or other structure that reminds people of an event or person

obelisk (OB-uh-lisk): a tall, four-sided piece of stone that has a pyramid shape at the top and is narrower at the top than at the bottom

INDEX

SHOW WHAT YOU KNOW

1. When did the Vietnam Veterans Memorial open?
2. What does the National Gallery of Art Sculpture Garden include?
3. What part does the National Park Service play in the upkeep of the National Mall?
4. What might you find in the Smithsonian Institution?
5. Name three monuments you can find at the National Mall.

WEBSITES TO VISIT

www.nationalmall.org/national-mall/explore-mall
www.nps.gov/nama/index.htm
www.si.edu

ABOUT THE AUTHOR

Joanne Mattern has written hundreds of books for children. Her favorite subjects are history, nature, sports, and biographies. She enjoys traveling around the United States and visiting new places. Joanne grew up on the banks of the Hudson River and still lives in the area with her husband, four children, and numerous pets.

Meet The Author!
www.meetREMauthors.com

PHOTO CREDITS: page 4 © Richard Semik; page 5 © Alex Gulevich; page 7 © Truchelut, Rue de Grammont Paris; page 8 © Napoleon Sarony; page 10, 11, 13, 14, 15, 17, 18, 20, 22 © Library of Congress; page 12, 16 © Statue of Liberty National Park Service; page 22 © Gustave Eiffel; page 23 © American Jewish Historical Society; page 24 © Edward Moran

Edited by: Jill Sherman

Cover design by: Nicola Stratford, nicolastratford.com
Interior design by: Renee Brady

Library of Congress PCN Data

National Mall / Joanne Mattern
(Symbols of Freedom)
ISBN 978-1-62717-739-9 (hard cover)
ISBN 978-1-62717-861-7 (soft cover)
ISBN 978-1-62717-972-0 (e-Book)
Library of Congress Control Number: 2014935664

Printed in the United States of America, North Mankato, Minnesota

Also Available as:

ROURKE'S e-Books